"Scott Silsbe is a poet who likes to tell stories. About his friends. The dive bars they haunt. The beers they drink. The road trips they take together. The strange and ordinary things they encounter. In his latest collection of poetry, *Meet Me Where We Survive,* there are multiple stories about all of the aforementioned. And should you wonder, dear poetry lover, yes, that is a good thing! These poems hum with a genuine wonder and appreciation for the quotidian, for what usually escapes unnoticed, "for paying attention to the conversation." "And I knew it wasn't an original thought," Silsbe confesses at one point, but who's complaining? So artfully direct are these poems they will surprise and disarm even the most cynical reader. "The singular imagination aims at producing / that which is both ephemeral and eternal." Scott Silsbe possesses such a "singular imagination." One you will find yourself returning to again and again." -Celeste Gainey, author of *the GAFFER*

Meet Me Where We Survive

Poems by Scott Silsbe

Kung Fu Treachery Press

Rancho Cucamonga, CA

Copyright © Scott Silsbe, 2022

First Edition: 1 3 5 7 9 10 8 6 4 2

ISBN: 978-1-952411-90-8

LCCN: 2021951434

Cover image: Jon Lee Grafton

Back cover photo: Joshua DeLisle

Ttile page image: Jason Baldinger

Author photo: Scott Silsbe

Acknowledgements:

Grateful acknowledgement is made to the editors of the following zines, journals, newspapers, or websites where earlier versions of these poems first appeared:

365 Poems in 365 Days, Alien Buddha Zine, As It Ought To Be, BBT Zine, The Beatknik Cowboy, Big Hammer, The Blue Hour, Chiron Review, Cultural Weekly, Duane's New Poe Tree, Gulf Stream, Lilliput Review, Nerve Cowboy, Nixes Mate Review, Pittsburgh Post-Gazette, Pittsburgh Quarterly, Pressure Press Presents, Pretty Owl Poetry, Red Flag, River Dog, Rust Belt Review, Rusty Truck, Rye Whiskey Review, Street Value, Trailer Park Quarterly, The Volta, and *WineDrunk Sidewalk.*

Two poems were featured in the anthology, *Recasting Masculinity.*
Three poems were also in *The Gasconade Review Presents: Strange Gods of the Prairie.*

Thanks to Jason Ryberg for all the hard work. And thanks to Jason Molina for the book's title.

Thank you, Jimmy Cvetic, for the encouragement—rest in peace, Jimmy.

Finally, thanks to Kristofer Collins, Jason Irwin, and Chandra Alderman for helpful editorial advice.

Table of Contents

I. Mount Trashmore

II. Poison Park

III. Shock Event

IV. Meet Me Where We Survive

for my parents

We believe too much in the singularity
of our own terrible hearts.

-Dave Newman

The world is awful
and we seem to enjoy it more all the time.

-Kristofer Collins

Mount Trashmore

Good Luck, Mr. Spy

for Gerald Stern

How young we all must have been back then. Was it
a quarter century ago? No. A mere decade. Or perhaps
a little more. I volunteered to drive my busted-up blue
Volkswagen out to the airport to pick you up. I wasn't
sure the car could make it, but I thought yes, perhaps,
if I coaxed it, if I said some sweet things to it, made it
some promises I was hoping I could keep. I knew that
my new friend Bob was a fan of your poems too and
I asked him if he would want to come with me to go
get you and he said that he'd love to. It seems to me
that it was winter. We were all wearing our big coats.
We looked like spies, you said. We got you back into
Oakland from the airport fine. I was pushing that VW
up Forbes Ave and I mentioned your old friend Jack
and you told me and Bob about how he used to jump
over the Cathedral hedges lining Forbes there, hurdle
them and sprint across the avenue. I think you told us
something about Billy Conn, The Pittsburgh Kid, but
I can't recall that story now. I remember that someone
that day asked you for advice, a young poet asking you,
the elder statesman, for some words of wisdom and that
you said to us, "Get your words out there. Don't wait."
You gave a talk. For some reason, I was shooed away
like a fly from dinner with you at the fancy restaurant.
But then you read to us. Some poems. And some essays
from your first essay collection. And later on there was

drink and food and more drink at Chuck's big old house.
At the end of the night, when the party dwindled down
and it was just some of us in Chuck's front room, you
and Chuck told stories back and forth. You told us about
your friend Louie saying, "What's this thing called dying
that we have to do?" And Chuck told a story about one
of his buddies picking a fight in a backwoods dive bar
and how he was scared because they were these giants,
these men his buddy wanted to fight. You said to him,
"Well, but Chuck, you're a pretty big guy yourself…"
and Chuck said, "Nah, man, these were Samoan cats."
And Diane snapped a picture of us there on the couch.
The last thing you said to me was to wish me good luck.
"Good luck, Mr. Spy," you said. And I've been meaning
to write this poem ever since. I thought it was a good title.
I thought, maybe, I might be able to make a poem out of it.

Double Downriver

I grew up on a dead end in the shadow of a trash dump.
It was not exempt from its own kind of magic though.

The dead end of the street gave way to an open field,
which led to a stand of trees bordering a skinny creek.
Bikes had forged a dirt path from the street to the creek
and there was an old cement culvert and old rope-swing
back among the trees a ways if you knew where to look.

On most Friday nights, we could all hear this great roar
of many car engines revving up down at the dragway,
even though it was a good two miles away from us.

When it would thunderstorm in the middle of the night,
we would wake up in the morning with booming heads,
lightning in our eyes, and all of the streets wiped clean.
The gulls squawking over the bulldozers on the dump.

How I Remember the Night Pavey Recited (from Memory) His Great Waffle House Poem in the Parking Lot of the Waffle House in (or Just Outside of) Blue Springs, Missouri

It was late, after a reading, and we poets were hungry.
We'd had milkshakes earlier for dinner, then beers or
shots or wine. And a lot of poetry. Perhaps too much.
And poetry can only satiate a certain kind of hunger.

And so the Waffle House sign hovering just off I-70
called out to us, was a sort of beacon in the night sky,
and our small caravan pulled off the freeway for grub.
We sat at the counter and the waitress was sweet to us.
I think we all ordered breakfast—several of us getting
their hashbrowns scattered, smothered, and/or covered.

It was clear the Waffle House chef took pride in his work.
Pavey covered the bill, saying that he knew it isn't easy
being a poor poet on the road. He was right about that.
And one last gift, before we headed our separate ways,
was a poem, recited from memory, in the parking lot,
there, with the cop cars, the holy Waffle House sign
above us—a poem about a Waffle House, of course.

And I can't recall how it went exactly, or even what
it was about, save that it mentioned a Waffle House.
But I think that I remember Pavey quoting scripture
in it, citing text some people believe came from some
great unseen, all-powerful, all-knowing force of life.

And for a moment, I believed in something greater than myself, the spirit moved me, there in, or just outside of, Blue Springs, MO in that Waffle House lot. I don't believe it was God I felt. I think it was poetry.

No Baby

My grandfather would keep us kids quiet by saying, "You're gonna wake the baby"—even when we all knew there wasn't a baby in the house. I was young and even though he was my grandfather, I couldn't get a good read on him—I didn't know whether or not he knew that there wasn't a baby in the house.

Bad Corner

The Take-a-Break Bar was a dive, but it had some charm to it. When you ordered a draft beer from the pretty barmaid, she'd always ask you if you wanted a "big one" and you always had to say yes. Regulars regularly sat around TAB's U-shaped bar and sometimes they got into verbal arguments with each other. There was this regular, a house-painter, I think, that Bob and I called The Bucket Guy. The Bucket Guy was one of the folks who seemed to get into verbal arguments with the other regs.

One night at the Take-a-Break, it was our bud Mark's birthday and all of his friends were filling him with shots and tall beers. At some point, we hoisted Mark up on our shoulders and sang "Happy Birthday" to him. And somebody grabbed one of the old Take-a-Break softball trophies off a corner shelf, passed it to Mark, and he hoisted it over his head as if he had just won it fair and square. And the pretty barmaid came running over to us and she said, "You can't do that. You gotta put that back." And she was right, of course, so we put the trophy back on its shelf and got Mark back down on the ground and we laughed at how stupid we all were, surprised she hadn't kicked us out.

If Sad Things Make You Sad

My friend Lori writes these poems—
they're beautiful and heart wrenching
at the same time. I don't quite know
how she does it. Just last night, some
of us went and saw her at a reading
down the street. My friends and I
went out drinking afterwards and
at one point, talking over Lori's
part of the reading, we decided
that she should give audiences
a trigger warning before she reads.
Something along the lines of
"If sad things make you sad,
you'll want to leave the room.
If sad things make you sad,
please, by all means, I think
that you should probably go."

Where's My Bucket?

Three men sit in the booth of a bar
drinking draft beers from pint glasses.
They make slow, deliberate movements.
They talk about books, music, and politics.
One of them says, "Let's prank somebody."
The others laugh, but he's serious about it.
A man named Elvis walks into the bar.
The merry prankster yells, "Elvis!" loud
enough that the man named Elvis hears
his name shouted over the bar-noise.
He sees the prankster and comes over
to the booth where the three men sit.
Elvis has half of a sandwich in a bag.
He's wearing a University of Pittsburgh
jacket and he tells the three men about
his job, about driving cross-country,
about what it feels like to find yourself
in an earthquake, grabbing for a tree
to stabilize yourself but realizing that
the tree is shaking and not stable either.
When Elvis leaves the table, the prankster
pranks a plumber, not knowing that he is
a plumber, yelling, "Where's my bucket?!"
into the phone. He pranks Jimmy, a retired
cop turned poet turned boxing instructor,
and says, "I had too many onion rings—

I just puked all over the bar. Pick me up!"
It's just this way with poets sometimes.
Sometimes the world that they live in
needs them to give it a little extra color.

My Favorite of My Grandfather's Jokes

So there was this guy driving down the road
and he saw a bar, so he stopped for a drink.
He got his drink and he was sitting there and
he saw another guy across the room and he
had a dog with him. So the guy is admiring
the other guy's dog and the other guy notices
and so he says, "Go on—call him on over."
So the guy calls the dog over and the dog
bites him. And so he looks at the other guy
and the other guy says, "He's not my dog."

Over the Median with Harry

It's after a reading at a little bookstore in Lawrence, Kansas.
People buying books. Poets trading books with each other.
A woman, maybe around my mother's age, approaches me
and introduces herself as Ronda. Ronda says she enjoyed
my reading, asks about a poem I read in which I mention
Harry Crews. "Are you a fan of Harry Crews?" she asks.
"I am," I say, "I'm a big fan of his memoir, *A Childhood.*"
"Well…" Ronda says to me, "Harry came and taught here
for a semester back in the day, when I was a student, and
I got all his books I could find and read all of them. So…
I got an idea of the kinda woman he liked from his books.
And when he came to teach, I arranged to have a meeting
with him in his office, and I wore my shortest skirt, and I
made a dramatic display of reaching for a book that was
high up on a shelf." "Alright," I said to Ronda. "And so,
that semester, when Harry gave his reading, there was
this large after-party, and when the party was over and
the people from the Department told Harry they were
gonna take him back to his hotel room, Harry pointed
at me and said, 'No, I'm goin' home with *her!*' And so,
I drove Harry to my place. He saw a liquor store along
the way and told me to pull over to it, but it was across
a median on the other side of the street so I said that I
couldn't—and Harry took the wheel and drove my car
over the median. So…I spent the next couple of days
with Harry, and the folks from the Department weren't
very happy with me because Harry wasn't supposed to

be drinking." This seemed to be where Ronda's story ended. I told her it was a great story and thanked her for it. "I called Harry in his later years," Ronda said, "since I heard his health wasn't good. I asked him if he would mind if I wrote about him…and Harry said to me then, 'As long as you're honest, you can write whatever you want.'" A good line. A great ending. Again, I think that Ronda is done. But then she says, "So I thought, you being a fan of Harry and all, you'd enjoy that story. And I know that now you'll probably go home and write a poem about how you met a lady who fucked Harry Crews, but I write poems too, so maybe I'll go home and just write that poem myself." "Well, alright," I said. And then Ronda went over to the bookstore counter and bought a copy of my book.

Reading Rich Gegick's *Greasy Handshakes* at Neighbors Tavern in Jeannette, Pennsylvania

Since it's my first time at Neighbors, I don't know what I want to drink. Call me a snob, but none of the drafts look appealing to me. But I order one anyway. I can't recall the last time that I had me a Coors Banquet beer. And it doesn't taste bad. But it doesn't taste great either—perhaps one of the worst things you can say about a beer. But I've got a copy of *Greasy Handshakes* and that is something. At the art gallery, Newman gave me a big box of them to take to Rich, his author copies. And I pulled one out of the box to have as a companion at the bar, promising I'd replace it after my brief stop off at Neighbors. Thinking maybe I'd only have to have one Coors Banquet if Bobby would be up for company once I am back in Allegheny County, and across the Westinghouse Bridge, where I feel at home, close to my lady and my friends and my collection of books and records, cassettes and compact discs and 8-tracks, DVDs and VHS tapes. I know I'm a sucker for crap. I fucking love crap. Maybe older crap especially, but any crap'll do. My crap. All that crap that I own. That crap almost makes you feel immortal, you know? I'm going to own all this crap forever. These records. These old-ass books. I didn't spill any of my Banquet on the book I borrowed, Rich. Next time I go to Neighbors, I think I'll get a bottle of High Life. Or else maybe I'll just stick to going to Johnny's Wife's Place.

A Poem About Mary for Renée

Renée, I never told you my stories about Mary.
And maybe you don't care about my stories
about Mary. But I wanted to tell them to you.
I'm not sure why I wanted to tell them to you.
Renée, I hope you don't mind me including
you in this poem. I guess maybe you'll never
see this poem, so I suppose it doesn't matter.

I think that I wanted to tell you about Mary
because I think you are a fan of her work.
And it's a nice or interesting thing to learn
personal anecdotes about people we admire.
It gives us a better sense of who they were
or who they are if they still inhabit this place.

Or maybe I wanted to tell you about Mary
because, in a way, she gave me a kind of hope
about certain things and it feels to me like
any kind of hope is worth spreading these days.
A poetry workshop can be such a deadening
kind of thing. In my experience anyway.
It can make a person feel like they never
want to write another poem or story again.
But Mary, she gave ours life. Even if only
because we didn't know what to expect,
we didn't know what she would say next.

Already the first day of workshop was unique.
As an icebreaker, Mary had us all go around
the room and try to recite the first line or two
of the first poem that we remembered writing.
My first lines were, "How do clouds stay up in
the sky? / They don't have wings, so we know
they don't fly." After we had gone all the way
around the room, Mary went around the room
again, addressing each poet, saying, "Scott—
your lines were about clouds up in the sky.
I think your poems are probably about you
observing the world around you and trying
to figure out how it works." She did that
for all of us poets, some 12 or 15 people.

One class, I turned in a poem that was not
very good. A grad student, I think his name
was Marcel, said something about my heavy
use of gerunds in the poem. And Mary said,
"Alright, everybody—ok, it's Gerund Day!
Every workshop I teach, there's one day
that is Gerund Day. Gerund Day, guys!"
I figured Mary would talk about gerunds,
what they are, how and when to use them
in our poems. But then she said, "Alright,
somebody tell me what a gerund is—I don't
know what it is except for that it's a rodent
that runs around a wheel in a little cage."
And my friend Amy said, "That's a gerbil."
To which Mary replied, "I know, I know."

In another class, we were all workshopping
a poem—and let's say it was by Marcel—
and the poem was entitled "Called Back."
"Before we begin discussing this poem,"
Mary said to us, "Someone tell us where
the title is from." The class was silent.
Mary asked us again—someone, anyone
say where it is this title is derived from.
Nothing. And so, reluctantly, Mary asked
Marcel, the author of the poem, to explain
where he got the title. "Well…there are
two different poets I like who have poems
with that title…I thought I'd try my own
hand at writing a poem with that title."
"And that's it?" Mary asked him sharply.
"That's it," Marcel said. At this point,
Mary seemed to begin talking to herself,
under her breath, with great incredulity.
She said something along the lines of,
"What's the state of poetry when poets
don't know what they're referencing
when then use something like this in
one of their poems? Do I just tell them?"
Then Mary stopped speaking to herself.
"'Called Back,'" she said to us slowly,
"are the two words…on the gravestone
of Emily Dickinson." She paused again.
"I don't have anything else to say about
this poem. Please go ahead and discuss."
I'm sure there are other stories I could tell.

I just wanted to tell you a couple, Renée.
I don't know now if they are worthwhile.
But I'm glad I told them. I like to think
that stories are important. In fact, I know
that stories are important. I know you've
got some good ones to tell as well. We're
all ears, Renée—make us laugh and cry.
Send us over the moon, why don't you?

Found Poem—Handwritten Sign Behind the Bar
at The Crystal Lounge in Alliance, Ohio

BUCKETS
ARE TO BE
DRANK THAT
DAY NO ROLL
OVERS OR
TAKEN HOME

Bill Fox's Guitar

I helped the guys from Cleveland load their gear up the stairs.
And up by the stage, one of them handed me Bill Fox's guitar.
I cannot remember now how it became clear to me that it was
Bill's guitar, but I want to say that it was passed to me almost
like a rather holy object and pretty much identified as such—
"This is *Bill's* guitar." I put it carefully in a corner of the stage.
And I looked at it. And I thought, "Most people would look at
that and think that it's just a guitar case. Just an ordinary case
for a guitar." But I had a deeper knowledge, an understanding
of what was in that guitar case and who the guitar belonged to.
And the songs that had been played on that guitar. Songs that
I knew, songs that I could sing. So I stood there and stared at
Bill Fox's guitar in the upstairs room of a bar in Pittsburgh—
imagining the rooms that guitar had been in, all of the nights
and stories and melodies that were the history of that guitar.
And I knew it wasn't an original thought. But because it was
Bill's guitar, it felt like something—like something special
or interesting or unique. Even though I knew that it wasn't.
But it felt like. And that feeling—that feeling was something.

Losing Something

Etched into
one of the
picnic tables
on the deck
out back at
Lou's Little
Corner Bar—
"Lou's Yourself."

The Nature of Things

I woke up holding the envelope, alive in my own bed.
She said, "Don't you have to go into work today?"
and I said, "I do. But I'm not in any hurry to go."
My friend drove me out to meet a stranger who said,
"You got a gift last night. I hope you realize that."
I'm not really sure how I was so lucky. But I was.
From here on out, I guess that I'll just dream dreams.

Mount Trashmore

Who wants this big
mound of garbage?

Every day it piles up
a little bit higher.

A sort of monument
of all of our waste.

It's got me thinking
about achievements.

What do you call the greatest
American accomplishment?

Our great contribution
to the world at large?

Perhaps the literature of
Whitman or Hemingway?

Maybe jazz or blues
or the game of baseball?

No, I'll tell you—
it's this here trash.

The great mound of it,
an astounding mountain.

America has produced
this mountain of trash.

Let's just build us a nice
ski slope on top of it.

Sterling State

for Pete Markus

I'm sitting here, drinking a beer, staring out
at the lake and the stacks of the nuke plant,
Pete, and I don't know why but I'm thinking
of you—of your voice, of your words, and
of the worlds that your words have created.
I've watched several big freighters pop up
on the horizon and then slowly disappear,
the sun glinting off the boats on the lake,
men and women, boys and girls biking
along the paved road skirting the beach.

Pete, I'm on my second beer and it's only
just past 1 in the afternoon. I like this kind
of day with this kind of day drinking. I saw
a sign on my way into this park that made
it sound to me like day drinking here might
be frowned upon. Maybe that just meant at
the beach. But I thought to myself that that
would be one rule I might have to break.

And Pete, I've been reading your new book,
the one about you teaching up in Detroit.
I'm only 50 pages in and it's a 200-pager,
but I'm only that far in because I'm really
savoring it. I like to save things for myself
that I know I will enjoy, you understand?

But the 50 pages I've read so far I've loved.
Already, I want to buy copies of this book
for everyone I know. I don't have the cash
in my bank account to buy copies for all of
the people I know though. So maybe one
at a time, as I get more money in the bank,
I will buy copies and distribute your book
to the world at large. As if my name were
Gideon and this here book of yours were
The Bible—The Good Book, as they say.
I think this book, it will do the world good.
I think this book, it's doing me some good.
I raise my early afternoon, day-drinkin',
frowned-upon brew to you, Petey-Boy—
thank you and congratulations, you dog.

One Night After Sandra Cisneros Gave a Reading in Pittsburgh

I drove Dave to the after-party in my busted-up old Volkswagen. The after-party was at a swanky house, owned by the head of the English Department, if I'm remembering right. And we drank up some fine red wine and ate up olives and little wedges of cheese.

This was years ago. I think I'm remembering this right. But I'm filling in some details, of course. But I remember Jeffy, who I'd always thought of as the department errand-boy, coming over to me at the party and asking me if I had driven there. And so I told him that I had. Jeffy said that they were looking for a way to get Sandra back to her hotel after the after-party was over. For some reason, I was selected. I told him I was happy to and I meant it.

I can see me and Dave and Sandra walking out to my shit-blue Volkswagen. Me and Dave drinky, embarrassed. Apologetic of ourselves a little, maybe. I don't know. I'm pretty sure the inside of the car was probably a mess and I had to do a hasty cleaning. Were we in Squirrel Hill? I want to say we were in Squirrel Hill. And Sandra's hotel was in Oakland. And I started up the Volks and we started to head towards Oakland, Sandra next to me up front and Dave starting his signature nod back in my backseat.

And Sandra asked us if there was any late night place to eat— she didn't have an appetite before the reading and the grub at the after-party wasn't substantial. I looked at Dave in the back and I said, "Ritter's?" The all-night diner was one of the only places in the city I imagined would be open. We wouldn't tell

Sandra that locals sometimes referred to the place as "Critters" due to the questionable cleanliness of the place. So Dave said, "Ritter's." And Sandra said an all-night diner sounded great.

We got Dave coffee to keep him from doing that good old nod. I ordered pancakes. Dave got pancakes. So Sandra followed suit. Three orders of pancakes. I can't remember if we played songs on the little table jukebox. But I know Sandra asked us about our writing—what we liked to write about, that kind of thing. I was surprised at her interest—her curiosity, her generosity in making us seem interesting. It actually seemed genuine.

After our breakfast, I drove into Oakland and we dropped Sandra at her big hotel. I think I opened the passenger side door for her. She gave Dave and I each a peck on the cheek and thanked us for the ride, the pancakes, and conversation. She went into her hotel and we drove off. I can remember Dave's big-ass, goofy grin, him shaking his head, laughing. I don't recall if he nodded off again before I got him home.

East Liberty Trumpet and The Wilkinsburg Whistler

Though I would prefer silence, I'll make the most of my time and try to get something down. Where do the mornings go? Most days to sleep. But I got a jump on the day and driving with the windows down through East Liberty caught a few stray notes from the guy who sometimes plays trumpet out in front of the Kelly-Strayhorn Theater. I wanted to stop to hear more, ask him what he's playing today. But there were books to sell, phone calls to receive, boxes to pack and ship.

The Wilkinsburg Whistler was walking up Hay this morning. Days when it's not too cold and not too hot and I can open up the loading bay door next to my desk at the warehouse, I can hear him coming from blocks away. Sometimes it isn't anything I can identify. Sometimes a standard, a classic tune, though with his own interpretation. Once, when John was out at the warehouse and we were working in the bay, we heard The Wilkinsburg Whistler coming in our direction, doing his version of "Summertime" and John said something like, "That's not quite how my version of 'Summertime' goes."

One Night at The Eclipse (Why Are You So Angry?)

Our friend was spinning records at this new place
none of us had been to before called The Eclipse.
The Eclipse was in what used to be a run down
part of town where it was cheap to live and drink.
But that part of town had become trendy and not
so cheap anymore. From the outside, The Eclipse
looked like an old man dive, glass cubes forming
the front window with a mess of Christmas lights
behind them. Inside, it was not an old man dive—
my beer cost me about 3 times what it should've,
there were a lot of college-aged kids in there, and
almost immediately upon entering the place, I felt
this odd sensation as if I had entered some other
dimension, some place I definitely did not belong.

I saw Joe sitting at a table at the back of the bar—
he waved me on over and I joined him at his table
which was right under the makeshift second floor
of the place. Joe and I didn't say much, just took in
the sights and sounds of the place. It became pretty
apparent to us that many people in the place were
on drugs of one kind or another, maybe a combo.

At one point, a girl descended the staircase that
spit out directly across from me and Joe's table
and the girl sort of hovered or flittered over to us

and put her hands on our table to steady herself. She struggled to make a sentence, sputtering out a partially-sensical string of noises that seemed to ask Joe and I what we were doing there or how we two knew each other. I explained to her that we were poets and had just come from a reading. "Imma poet," our new friend told us, "My friends say…that I'm a beat-neck." This made her laugh.

Another girl floated down the staircase and over to our table next to the beat-neck. Looking at her beat-neck friend, she slurred, "What even are you doing down here? Who are these guys anyway?" It was at this point the newcomer turned to look in the direction of Joe and she must have seen his aura or something. Without Joe even saying anything to her, the girl asked Joe, "Why are you so *angry?*" And Joe replied sternly, "I'm not angry." But she wouldn't accept it. She was certain Joe was angry. And so she convinced her friend to join her out on the back deck of The Eclipse, away from Joe and his angry face. And so Joe and I sipped our overpriced beers and listened to old soul songs and I decided that I would enjoy myself there at the mystical Eclipse as I would probably not be returning any time in the foreseeable future.

Rumblestrip

I can still see us there, in winter, huddled together—
not due to the cold, but because of the pick-up truck
driving the Bloomfield Bridge, honking at us lovers
there on the rumblestrip near where the driver was
merging onto the bridge, no doubt in disbelief that
we two were there on the bridge and at that late hour.
Even if I could have said something to him by way
of explanation, I'm not sure what I would have said.
"It's all her fault," perhaps? Or maybe, "We're drunk."
We were definitely coming back from a Polish Hill bar.
I don't recall how drunk we were. Somehow we'd been
stranded without a car or a ride back to one of our cars
and so we decided to walk, through the snow and cold
of Polish Hill and Bloomfield, to her apartment, I think.

And I pointed us in one direction, and she pointed us
in another, and she insisted, so we took her way, which
left us under the Bloomfield Bridge, looking up at it,
knowing it was our way back, then trudging up the slope
through the snow and dead plants and weeds and leaves.
I'd put money on that she didn't have the right kind of
shoes for such adventurous hiking. But we made it up
to the bridge, hopped the wall and landed there, I think,
on that rumblestrip, just in time for the passing driver
to lay into his horn. There's a lot I don't remember now.
But I remember that. And I can easily access how I felt.
I was in love with her. And I was uncertain whether or

not she was in love with me. But that second part didn't really matter to me. Only my love for her mattered then. I had no control over the other thing. And I thought that my feeling was strong enough for us both. I was wrong.

To the Guy at Primanti's Who Wanted to Talk Politics with Me

I get it. You're lonely. You want some dinner conversation.
But I didn't come here for conversation. I came here—plain
and simple—for a sandwich. One with fries and slaw on it.

You really want to know, I'll tell you my opinion here, now.
Though I highly doubt you will ever read this poem. I think
our country is lacking in empathy at the moment and I have
empathy for those who take offense to monuments depicting
men who would kill others for the right to own other people.
I see no problem. Bring them on down. Fuck the confederacy.

Jack Gilbert (1925-2012)

When I was 18 years old and knew next to nothing
about poetry besides Bill Wordsworth and Ed Poe,
my composition teacher passed a photocopy of one
of your poems out to our class and it changed my life.
I knew I hadn't ever read a poem quite like it before.

It seemed like everywhere I went, I found your words.
Another teacher, face full of awe, recited to our class
your lines, "I say moon is horses in the tempered dark
because horse is the closest I can get to it." Leaving us
all speechless. Nothing left to do but dismiss class then.

Some years later, a friend told me that he'd heard you
were living in Massachusetts—unsure whether or not
your poems were being read and unsure whether or not
people cared about your work. I resolved to look you up,
find you, and let you know just how important you were.

And you were not that hard to find. On a business trip,
I went out of my way to find the street in Northampton
a computer said you lived on. I found the house, parked,
knocked on the door, and the man who came to the door
told me you lived up over his garage—he invited me in.

The first thing you said to me was, "Why are you here?"
I tried to say something about being a fan of your work.
But you said, "No, why are you *really* here?" And I said,

"Well, because I'm…a poet." And you said, "That's right,
you have to say it." And you asked me where I was from.

I said I was up from Pittsburgh, but that I was born in Detroit.
You said, "Well…that's like jumping from one smokestack
to another." You asked me why I wanted to be a poet. I told
you I just wanted to write good poems. "What about fame,"
you asked me, "Or money?" "No," I said, "Just good poems."

You asked me to read you some of my poems. I admitted
to being a little nervous. "I know," you said, "I was nervous
when I went to visit Pound in the castle. But Pound told me
then that he was done reading the work of younger writers…
so you can't do a whole lot worse than that." You were right.

So I read you some of my poems. And we talked them over.
You asked to keep them, saying, "Write your name on them."
I asked if you thought you'd publish another book of poems.
And you said, "I didn't think so," pausing, "But my ex-wife
Linda calls me every day and tries to convince me I should."

A few months after my visit, I wrote you a letter of thanks.
I sent you a few of my newest poems. Several months later,
I got a postcard from you, telling me you were working on
a new book of poems. It was to be our first and last bit of
correspondence. You said, "I liked saying something most."

Poison Park

Singing in the Shower

Sometimes I recognize that you will forget me,
that we will forget all of this, and that all of this
will forget us, that we ever inhabited this space.

But these days, I find that when I'm not thinking
about the present or the past, I'm often thinking,
"Don't think that—just please don't think that."

I slice open my middle finger while chopping up
vegetables for dinner. Maybe it was an accident.
Maybe I wanted some outward display of what's
inside me. Maybe it's a little "fuck you" to myself.

It just feels like I've been so damn malleable lately.

I call up my mother to let her know I'm not "dead
on the side of the road," as she seems to like to say.
She tries to comfort me by saying she thinks we've
avoided something worse, something like a civil war.
She means well, but it's not much of a comfort to me.

But I think about D.H. Lawrence, how he said that we
have "to live, no matter how many skies have fallen."
I put on John Coltrane records until I've run through
all my John Coltrane records, then start back at the top.
And that seems to do some damage. It seems to tame
the beast a little. I think I'm good to step outside and
confront the world. I'm getting ready and I'm singing.

Looking for Richard Brautigan in
Pittsburgh, Pennsylvania in 2018

The stone hits hard against the pavement—
it could be there is no luck to be had anymore.

I just now started to worry about solar storms,
not knowing what they are. Something about
the heliosphere, a disturbance in space weather.

But I also just started to surrender myself
to whatever it is the universe has to shell out.

Icy moons spewing water plumes—I surrender.

Bungee-jumping neo-Nazis—I surrender.

Japanese hot tub monkeys—I surrender.

I surrender myself to the radio galaxies,
the blazars I can't comprehend, and all of
the artificial satellites in retrograde orbits.

I can't make sense of all the things I don't understand.

If you happen to see Richard around town,
point him in my direction, wouldn't you?

Waiting in Line at the Post Office

I know that
there are fates
worse than this,
but right now,
at this moment,
I can't name them.

I have this thought
and then I realize
what an asshole
I must be to have
this kind of thought.

There are terrible
things happening
to many people
all across this
planet right at
this very moment.

There are awful
things that people
are doing to each
other. So many
awful things,
in fact, that
at times I'm

embarrassed
to call myself
a human being,
to lump myself
in with others.

But there are
also good things
people are doing
for each other
and I try to focus
on that, try to
concentrate on
the positive,
so I don't fall
down deep
into a well
of despair
or become
one of those
people who
are always so
cynical and
sinister, so
negative that
it becomes
their main
attribute or
their main
world-view.

But still, I try
to keep in mind
the awful things,
keep them not
too far away,
so as not to be
too delusional.
This world,
in my opinion,
already has
plenty of that.

I Fucked Up

I fucked up.
I got fucked up.
I broke down.
I got broke.
There was everything.
Then nothing.
Then nothingness.
Then mere being.
I had a crisis.
I had a car-crash.
I was all alone.
Then I was not alone.
I was alive.
I was also on fire.

North Dixie Highway

I was driving down Dixie
closing in on the freeway,
and coming towards me,
a guy on a red mo-ped—
left hand steering but
with a cigarette between
two of his fingers,
right hand holding
a flip-phone to his ear,
the two stacks of Fermi,
the nuclear power plant,
looming just behind him.

Blessing

A man has found the woman he was looking for.
She is Saint Bridget of Sweden. When he
followed her to the monastery at Vadstena,
the forests marked Xs on his hands.

The flowers in the man's buttonholes have faded.
Bridget is calling the blue-heads from the trees
to the grass, her hands full of her own hair.

The man approaches Bridget. She is talking
to herself. She is talking to Saint Francis.
She is only sometimes completely alone.

Mercy, the man says, and Bridget listens.
Mercy, the man says. And Bridget responds.
The soul is a dirty rag, she says.

Once a crucifix spoke to Bridget. And several times,
the man dreamt of Bridget, telling her
to wait, he had something for her.

But then, this is different.
It was a long trip back from Compostela, she says.
The first visions were slowly coming back.

Bridget begins recounting her revelations.
The clouds overhead resemble soldiers
and horses. The man turns and walks back toward
the forest. He doesn't notice the Xs vanishing from his hands.

Poison Park

I can't see the hill from here. This isn't the place I remember calling my home. But maybe I was just delusional before this. It feels to me that now the world is half-mad half of the time and more than half-mad the rest of the time. Cruel and selfish people who opt to look the other way when it's convenient for them to do so are allowing some to take advantage, making it harder on those who are struggling, adding strife to their lives. But I am doubtful I can convince him that life is not just some kind of a business transaction. Or that it's too small of a planet for that kind of talk. That it could very easily get us all killed.

My friend Meghan says she doesn't believe in God, but that she puts her faith in people. And so when something like this happens, it makes her question her faith. People are so awful. Maybe Jimmy was right when he said that the world is ending. Someone burnt out the old cork. Perhaps humanity's jumped the shark. Our dignity slowly sliding away. It's so painful see it. I want to believe I can make a difference, but I'm discouraged. I got nothing. At night, I try to sleep and all I hear is a noise that sounds like some music from the other side of the moon. The last time was the last time. The dogs, they go with me.

The Tracks

after Tranströmer

Moonlight at 2 a.m. There's a train that is stopped
in an open field. Shards of light from a distant city
are cold as they flicker on the far horizon.

Like when a person goes into the depths of a dream
so far, they don't ever remember they were there
once they've made it back to their bedroom.

Or when somebody falls into a deep sickness
and all of their days turn into flickering shards,
swarming, cold and faint off on the horizon.

The train sits there completely still. 2 a.m.
The moonlight strong. Only a few stars.

Just As Long As I'm in This World

Is there anything else I can do
to relieve this nagging sense
of regret mixed with a touch
of fear of the unknown future?
Maybe I should see someone.
But I feel like I know too many
people already. They crowd
my daily life—I feel I am too
infrequently completely alone.
But this sinking feeling I have.
I think I need to do something
about it. Maybe it's just what
all of us feel. Or maybe it's a
genetic thing. Maybe I should
listen to more blues records—
"I am the light of this world."

The Blue Cloak

Though no one else in the scene seems to notice them,
    the viewer's eye
is drawn to them, focuses on them, and cannot help
    but return to them.
She in her long, red gown putting the blue cloak on
    him, wrapping him
in it, nearly about to pull the wool over his eyes. He
    doesn't seem to see.
She's blinding him. And I'm not sure, but I believe it's
    her cloak, isn't it?

They're center stage in a crowded landscape, in a sea
    of other proverbs,
other sayings or expressions. To their left, a pig is
    being slaughtered—
what does that one signify? A pig is always stabbed
    through the belly
with a knife? The die is cast. And to their left a man
    shovels dirt into
a well that bears a dead calf—after a disaster, an action
    must be made.

In Hogenberg's engraving from 1558, a year before
    Bruegel's painting,
he represented over 40 proverbs, including the woman
    and her blue cloak.
Bruegel's painting has over 100—but the blue cloak is
    more pronounced.

What did Bruegel see in the blue cloak? Why did
    he make it so central?
Perhaps he felt there was a cloak of deceit he was
    being wrapped up in.
Not necessarily by an unfaithful wife. It could be
    the uncertainty of his
times made him fear he could not distinguish
    true light from false light.

An early title of the painting used the phrase
    "The Folly of the World."
An alternate title was "Topsy-Turvy World"—the
    world upside-down.
The proverbs come-to-life act out our human
    foolishness, all the ways
we fall prey to the stupidity and vanity of the
    world we have created.

The painting hangs in Berlin. I wonder if some 20
    years ago I walked
past it. I can't recall now. I would not have know
    much of Bruegel—
I wouldn't have known anything about the woman
    and her blue cloak.

Rats

after Trakl

Out in the courtyard the autumn moon is shining.
Fascinating shadows fall from the edge of the roof.
A great silence takes up residence in the windows.
And underneath them, rats have quietly appeared.

They squeak and scamper around here and there
and a there is a hazy, gray stench that seems to
have followed them down from the outhouse,
the ghostly light of the moon trembling a little.

And the rats scurry around with crazy greed
and crowd all of the houses and the barns
that are packed full with fruit and with grain.
The ice-cold winds groan in the darkness.

Mail-Ladies

Inside Noah's black and white corner diner,
the man who rang the bell when he came through
the door asked the blue woman if she would be
his mail-lady and, as she declined, the man across
the counter went on asking himself where he lived
and if he could ever possibly have a blue mail-lady.

The Color Only Found in Caves

for Phil Geist

It isn't something I'm sure I can properly articulate.
A sort of struggle between my mouth and my mind.
Either it's getting better or I'm just growing used to
the pain. Baldinger says that we are all getting old
and weird and we were already weird to begin with.
Look at us with our brand new medical conditions.

People regularly disappoint me. Even those closest
to me. Maybe especially those who're closest to me.
I disappoint myself too—but I forgive myself easily.

I'm too in love with certain things of this world—
and I know that. That young student who snorted
when she laughed. Or the boathouse on the river
that my old teacher Petey pointed out to me while
we were out on his Boston Whaler. Or else the box
of letters I have sitting on a shelf, waiting for me.

And stories—I love a story with a surprise ending.

Phil told us the story of how once, when he was
a child, he was climbing a tree and his grandfather
saw him, but instead of yelling at him for doing it,
which Phil thought he was going to, he yelled up
at him, "Keep on going—you're almost at the top!"

Spring Vigil in the Imperial Chancellery

after Tu Fu

Flowers lurk on the dusk of a palace wall.
Birds, coming to nest, pass by in a *chiu, chiu.*
The stars come on like ten thousand households,
move beside the moon in nine skies or more.
Those not asleep hear golden keys because
of the wind. They think of jade pendants, of
tomorrow morning, or of business deals they've
sealed. How many times will they ask the night?

My Pale Blue Heart

for Meghan Tutolo

I've never seen the thing, but it's in there—
oh baby, I know it. I can feel that it's there.
Couldn't tell you why it's pale blue though.
That's a mystery. Because I'm cold as ice?
Because I'm an Aquarius and love to swim?
Or because I'm a sucker for a good moon?
Why is anything the shade it appears to be?
Because of refracted light, I suppose. Right?
I'm okay with my heart being pale blue.
Makes me feel like a blue-blood—fancy!
Most days I feel pale blue. What's in
your heart? What color's your blood?

A Note to Benger, Way Out in Kansas

And it is quite a ways. I know—I've done
the drive. Well, to Kansas City at least.
Never been to Lenexa. How is Lenexa?
Benger, I am here with your chapbook
next to me and I have just read one called
"A Crack in Her Teacup." I've finished
my lunch, on break from work. This is
a lunch poem, I guess. I decided to have
me a beer with my lunch. Because I can,
because it's almost Independence Day,
because I'm feeling kind of free, I guess.
Benger, the beer tastes good, but I have
to go back to work very soon, I'm afraid.
Benger, I hope you'll keep pounding that
page and I will keep at it too. This isn't
much of one, but you'll have that—there
will be some duds. Add it to the Mount.
Tried out one this morning that I called
"Writer's Block Does Not Exist." Not
sure it is a very good poem, but, well,
I dug the title and message. Sometimes
you've gotta write yourself a bad poem
with a good title. All else be damned.

The Lonely Volunteers

"I don't know why we do it. We must be crazy."
                                        -Richard Hugo

There isn't any real point in questioning why we do it.
It's a lonely craft, for sure. It alienates the most social
of us. But it's some sort of odd compulsion, I suppose,
to put down words like this, try to articulate the thing.

Richard—I think of you and your fine poems all about
Montana and Italy, bars and loneliness and your friends.
I think that your friends called you "Dick," but you died
when I was just four years old, so we two never met, we
never became friends, so I think that I'll stick to Richard.

I'm not sure what I would say to you if I had the chance.
I suppose that I'd thank you for your poems. It's funny,
isn't it, how we feel a gratitude for the work of others?

But your poems have enriched my life—that's the way
I think about it. You once wrote, "You have to be silly
to write poems at all." And I can see that. It's ridiculous.
So is writing a poem to a dead man who'll never read it.
I don't know why I do it. I must be crazy. But maybe,
it's something very human—this urge to communicate
with someone who isn't around anymore. And maybe
it's one of the things we do that is odd, but endearing.

I don't know for certain, Richard, but I think that maybe, you might understand me when I say that lately I find it difficult to tune into the nightly news report, to learn of the many horrors human beings are capable of these days. I want to scream obscenities at the television, but I know that wouldn't help. And I don't know what would help.

So I switch the machine off. And I pull your books down off the shelf, sit with you a while. And you make me want to try harder. To get better. To be better. And to accomplish something with this, the only life I know that I will ever have. I feel lonely because of your poems. And I thank you for that.

My Grandfather Discusses Fire

"There's something about it," he said,
while shifting the logs of the fire around
with a stick. And we just stared into it,
all silently watching. He said, "You see?"

Disintegration

There are
few times
I am more
enamored
with my life,
more grateful
for everything,
than the moment
on those days
after a night
of heavy drinking
when a serious
and painful
hangover
somehow,
miraculously,
loosens its
grip and lifts,
disintegrating
like smoke
or mist over
the rooftops
of some tiny
city that is
under the
assumption
it will
go on
existing
forever.

Things That Happened Once

after Rodney Jones

I remember there was this one night
that my father sang Tina Turner's
"What's Love Got To Do With It"
at Nico's Recovery Room karaoke.
He sang it so quietly into the mic,
I had to run up there to help him,
making the song a father-son duet.

To the Saint After He Had Found His Glasses

for Tomaž Šalamun

I wish I had some stories.
Or even just one, really.
Though I suppose there are
plenty of stories in the world.

It's the day after New Year's Day
but we are not in New Zealand.
I fell asleep to the tune of
an old Marx Brothers movie.

But what was I saying here?
Something about your life.
I didn't know you very well.
We talked poetry, I believe.

I can think of a small reading
at a very bad Italian restaurant.
And can hear your voice, but
cannot think of what you said.

Robert called you the saint
after he had found his glasses.
The statue of the saint inside
the church on a winter's night.

People meet people every day.
This is a remembrance to a saint
with glittering eyes and glasses
from a stranger, or damn near.

In Moments

for Don Wentworth

We were out in Jeannette on a Friday night
and Don was talking about the night before.
He said, "There were these moments…"
and I can't remember whether or not
he used the word "transcendent,"
but he very well might have.

But anyway, I knew what he meant.
I might've tried to articulate the same
kind of thing to Bob as he left my place
one night after we had a good practice.
I can almost hear us there on the porch,
Bob saying, "It sounded good tonight,"
and me replying, "There were moments."

To Be Simple Again

for Chandra

Tonight, in the basement, it was just me and
Jason Molina, and his guitar, and the cricket
in the window, and the beer can, and the pipe.
Somewhere, out in the night, were my friends
and, further out, my sister and even further out,
my folks, out across the ocean far out and away.
But I was just down in my basement with Molina
on the stereo and Chandra on the internet wires
saying digitally that she would write me a good
old-fashioned analog letter through the good old
United States Postal Service, a stamp on it and all,
a forever stamp that will no doubt be good forever.
What else will be good forever? Tonight, I drove
through Pittsburgh Friday early-evening rush hour
to see Dan out at the Buddha in the North Hills,
drove with the windows down, enjoying the cool
the rain had put in the air. Upon returning home,
I found the house empty—a quiet, empty house
on a Friday night. And so I cracked open a beer
and listened to a 7-inch that Mark had given me—
spinning it twice, as if I felt I had missed something
the first time. I looked at the water tower Dan drew
and I drank my beer and I listened to Mark's record.
And I guess I got lonely for company because then
I was on the internet wires looking for someone to
talk to and I found Eli and told him about the books

of James Crumley, and I found Matt and I told him that I would meet him for day-drinking at Howard's. And then I didn't want much more than Molina's voice on my basement stereo, singing how this whole life has been about trying to be simple again. He said it like this: "Try and try and try / And try and try and try.... / To be simple again." And I spun the full band version first with the sad and lonesome lapsteel and then I put on the demo that's just Molina's voice and his guitar and it was more sad and lonesome and it sounded so good that it hurt a bit and I missed Molina and was sad that he's gone and it was more complicated than that but I didn't know quite how to express it, so I picked up a guitar and tried to learn his song, knowing I could never sing it like him, but not caring, and I crooned as best I could for the cricket in the window and the world that was up in flames outside the basement walls trying as hard as it could to self-destruct, but I still promised Chandra that I would write her back before too long once I got her letter.

Shock Event

Red Lightning

A sprawl of light takes over the night's horizon.
The authorities are quick to shoot down theories
that it's something otherworldly or problematic.

There isn't very much below us or above us—
it turns out we were short-sighted once again.
Talking to no one—or else myself—I say,
"I'm going to have nightmares tonight."

But, then, this isn't about me. It's about us.
All of us. We're in this damn thing together.
It seems to me that we forget that these days.

She suggested we sit and watch the country
burn and destroy itself—the way we knew
it always would. I guess I hadn't realized
that it would be televised. But there it was.

For a moment, I think a little about the things
I would save if I could save them. Even though
it's pointless. Even though they're already gone.

What I Am Going Through

The high winds knocked the power out—it popped back on
a few times for a bit and then it was gone. Perhaps for good.
I left the house not knowing how it would be upon my return.

These days, I can't seem to look people in the eye when they
ask me how I'm doing. I don't think that it's that I'm not well—
it's just that it's such a personal question. But I could be wrong.

I told my friend that my lady can't stop checking on the news
and he said, "She has a problem." And I said to him, "We all
have a problem." I don't know if he understood what I meant.

When I'm out on the water, things don't seem so bad to me—
I'm not sure if it's that the river is calming to my sensibilities
or if I just enjoy the isolation, the distance from other people.

Before the light of this day is gone, I hope to have a new way
of thinking. At the very least, a different emotional zip code.
The laughter only makes it burn more. Don't moan so much.

Driving Around Pittsburgh Through an Early
March Snow Listening to the Jimmy Woods
Sextet's *Conflict*

The singular imagination aims at producing
that which is both ephemeral and eternal.
At least I think that's what Bachelard meant.

Today I drove while white fluff piled up
on my windshield and on the sidewalks
and streets and the roofs of the buildings
around me and while somehow, recordings
of songs from some fifty-five years ago
made their way through the stereo system
of my beat-up, silver bullet of a minivan.

And it didn't matter how much time was left.

One Night at Mariani's Pleasure Bar with Bart Solarczyk

All of my memories are going—but I think I still have a few.
We went to a reading at the old Book Exchange or The Whale,
stopping off at your car for a little smoke and some Son Volt,
then walking the couple of blocks back to Liberty and the bar.
I think I ordered an Oberon draft and I think you followed suit.
The bartend asked if we were eating and you said you'd look
at a menu. And I think eventually you ordered fried calamari
for us to share. I know that we talked about the small press—
of your memories of the '80s and '90s when Nimmo was still
up in Detroit, and Mark Weber was around, and Androla was
still reading out, and Harry Calhoun did his *Pig in a Poke* or
Pig in a Pamphlet. I think you told me again about how you
have a bin or two of correspondence and old zines and mags,
your letters from Judson Crews, your copy of the Bukowski
chapbook that Nimmo published. How you'd have to crack
those open some day to show me. Stories about the old days.
The night Zen snuck the nitrous tank into Hemingway's Bar
for the reading in the back room, how some of the wait-staff
were hitting the tank too and fucking up everybody's orders.
And maybe you told me the story of your 40th birthday party.
It's kind of blurry. But that's what I think I can remember.
Us drinking at the bar at Mariani's. Surrounded by overhead
television screens telling us what was going on in the world
beyond the glass windows of the bar. And us ignoring them.
Not wanting that information—not caring about it one bit.
Paying attention to the conversation. The stories. Our beers.

I Must've Left My Heart My Heart in Pittsburgh

My heart, my heart—
it repeats in these thumps
or iambs in Pittsburgh,
city of bridges, city of
steel, city of poetry.

That One Morning

That one morning
I tried to wake her
by whispering
through her
bedroom window,
Dear One,
Sweet One,
Honey, Baby,
Dearest,
Sweet Thing—
wake up.

The Pair

after Tranströmer

They switch off the lamp and its white bulb glows
for a bit before it dissolves, as if it were a tablet
in a glass of darkness. And then they are lifted.
The walls of the hotel push up into the dark sky.

Their passionate jostling slows and they fall asleep,
but somehow, their most secret thoughts meet up,
like when two colors collide and mix together
on the paper of a schoolchild's wet painting.

It's dark and quiet. But tonight, the city—with
its switched-off windows—is pushing in close.
Houses have come. They stand packed together,
a crowd waiting there with expressionless faces.

What Happened There

What happened there in the dark
or perhaps with all the lights on
in some strange room somewhere
without inhibition, and gleefully,
perhaps we will never really know.
I do remember several things from
the night in question, but loosely.
A heavyset man dancing erotically
and recklessly with the main pole
of a large tent as if he were a stripper,
nearly bringing it all down with him.
Riding backwards in a golf cart
down dark, unknown dirt roads
a colorful hat flying off one of
our heads, off into the night and
its dark and the trees and the dirt.
A drunk couple getting booted from
a family restaurant for "language"
and the ensuing disappointment of
the others of us sitting at the bar.
And you, pounding on the door
of our room, angry with me,
incredulous that I had not let
you in the room any earlier—
somehow suggesting that I was
responsible for you being locked
out of the room, your pinky toe

damaged somehow in the night.
Thinking about it now, I wonder
what it was you were looking for
out there in the world beyond our
makeshift bedroom, what signal
in your brain got you out of bed
and wandering outside the door.
When I asked you in the morning
what you were doing in the middle
of the night, you said, "Sleeping."

The Trumpets

after Trakl

Under the clipped willow trees where children play
and leaves are tumbling around blow the trumpets.
There's a great quaking in the church's graveyard.
Red flags rifle through the suffering of the maples
as people ride alongside open fields and empty mills.

Or else the shepherds who sing all night as deer enter
the circle of their own fires, the grove's age-old grief.
A group of dancers who flail against the black wall.
Red flags, loud laughter, craziness, and the trumpets.

Box of Letters

I don't know what I'm saving it for.
But I have it stashed on what I think
is a safe spot—next to my old Exley,
below the clipped quote from Proust,
and by the drawing of Richard Yates.
But yes, those letters are there for me.
For someday. For I don't know what.

Inventory

Not enough humanity,
not enough generosity.
Too much willful ignorance.
Too much hatred and scorn.
And all of it all the time
on every channel
and in every language.

Nothing sacred.
Nothing justified or clarified.
Nothing doing, really.
Nothing much of anything
that any of us care about
save more of the same bullshit
or else a punch in the face.

Early November

Leaning out of my upstairs bathroom window,
I watch the crows follow each other, en masse,
from Garfield toward downtown into the sunset.

Poem for Demetrius M. Salada, Admiral (RA) of the Golden Arc Spaceship

Admiral Salada, I don't know if it's really true—
if the Golden Arc that you built got you to space.
By chance, I found myself in a small apartment
in Braddock Hills sifting through what remained
of your library—books rescued, I was told, from
a house fire. Some of the better titles I noticed…
Experiences of Space in Contemporary Physics.
The Harmonics of Sound, Color, and Vibration.
Extraterrestrial Contact and Human Responses.
Effects of Nuclear War on the Pittsburgh Area.

The man who was selling the books handed me
your old business card, which is how I know of
The Golden Arc. That and his story about how
you just vanished one day after years and years
of telling people that you were building yourself
a way to leave this cracked earth, this busted world,
this unsustainable planet we're breaking to shards.

I hope that your spaceship held up and got you
to wherever it was that you were heading for.
I now keep your business card in my wallet as
a conversation piece, as a souvenir from my job
to show off to people I meet. And I guess as a
small piece of your life, which I know little of—
just a small fragment from someone who had hope
of another world that was obtainable, if very distant.
Someone who didn't care if people thought he was
stupid, crazy, or a dreamer of otherworldly dreams.

Handwritten Sign on the Door
of Valley Sales & Service

Wilkinsburg, PA

Closed til further notice—
Jim broke his ankle-bone.

It's Not the End of the World (How Do You Know?)

There's a national change shortage. And there's too much information on the second floor—they've had to post signs around the building that say, "Notice of Imminent Danger." They have different procedures in place for what they call the High-Risk Long-Term Unemployed. I believe that the syndrome has a new name now, but it used to be referred to as Great Depression Mentality. This was all linked to actions taken by Late-Stage Disaster Capitalists. My god in heaven.

In Defense of Escapism

A woman drops a coin on the ground and a pigeon
gobbles it up. The pigeon loses feathers in the cracks
of the sidewalk and fire hydrants sprout from the pavement.

The shoes of old men are reflected in the mirrors
of the dead. And at night, the dead slip the shoes
on their own hands and walk upside down until morning.

There are streetlamps tied into the city's hair and they flash
out over the darkness like candles flickering inside of bodies.

The skyscrapers are growing restless. They crowd together
by the edge of the river and the lights in their windows
shine on the water's surface, glinting off the walls of waves.

Someone's replaced the moon with a graphite ball. Orion shoots
a chisel with his bow and graphite shards break open the sky.

The world is enough for everyone and there is
a flame for each of us in every world other than this.

Chautauqua

The bell tower on the pier chimed ten times
as I walked toward it with my guitar in hand.

The rickety old wooden dock on the lake
was completely covered in white bird shit.

The crow on the black peak of the roof
of the house cawed twice with great force.

There was a rising hum overhead—
it did not sound like an airplane to me.

Loss

I'm fairly certain
I've already forgotten

some of those
little things

I promised myself

I would
never forget.

It's a shame, but
nothing's permanent.

Confessionalism

My heart is growing
a little bit smaller
with each passing day.
I know I shouldn't
talk about it.

Water Tower

Night under the water tower. Something goin' on up the street.
There are flashing lights, sirens—the whole area blocked off
to thru traffic. And I think I hear screaming for some reason.
In the dark, the big blue water tower up over Garfield feels like
it's some sort of artifact lending hints to the origin of the moon.
And the light pouring out of the windows of houses on the hill
might be the visible hearts of people from an underground city.
Guitars and amplifiers and effects-pedals are stringing together
an outer space type of music that the neighbors are noticing—
new songs are being created in small bedrooms and basements
of row houses on alleys with names like Almond and Decision.
Down the hill, the long hallways of shotgun apartments lean to
the street as if the years have conjured a desire in them to leave.
And all the stars in the night sky just beyond the streetlights are
a new history or a slow fire that are most likely dead on arrival.
We may never know what it is that's happening up the street—
what new dark gravity is taking hold. Could be that someone
got a little careless letting the devil out. But we stay on, keep
inhabiting this space. I don't know what others are looking for
moving to places that are not here. The mountains are pretty,
but I don't need the mountains—I have the clouds and rivers.
I have the tunnels and the bridges. And anyway—how do you
expect to get anywhere when you never stay in the same place?

Two Large Plastic Cups from Bojangles

Driving back from visiting my parents
in Carolina—on the side of the road,
two large plastic cups from Bojangles
rolling around in the highway breeze
like a pair of Southern tumbleweeds.

We're All Lonely, Jay

She took up running—some kind of health kick.
I think she wanted to reinvent herself. Or her life.
This was in our last couple of months together.
Before we split up. I never even got a chance
to ask her what it was that she was running from.

Path of the Flood

We're all singin' a song that Bobby wrote—"22 is a road,
not a gun…"—and talking about strip clubs, which ones
are gone forever, which ones are still standing but empty,
closed, with future uncertain. We can't remember if it was
Cheaters or Streakers that was up on Route 30. "Streakers
is for sale, I think," one of us says. And Bobby tells us all
about the drive-thru strip club that he drove through once.
We pass a place called Nanty-Glo and I say, "Nanty-Glo"
out loud just to say it and I hear JB in the passenger seat
say it too. I suppose people like us just like to say things.
This here is a road trip during a pandemic. We won't be
able to see the insides of buildings, but we're going up
to where the old manmade lake was, to follow the path
of the flood down to where it destroyed the city, then
go up the hill to where the dead of the flood are buried.
On the drive back, we pass the Jonnet Flea, a giant old
flea market building, where people are setting tables up
out front. JB says he once got some old newspapers there
about The '77 Flood. He says he'll show them to us sometime.

Meet Me Where We Survive

She Got My Mind Messed Up

It's what I don't want to talk about.
It's what I don't understand, or else
what hurts me, and so, what I avoid.
I would rather discuss how good that
handcabbage is from the new Chinese
restaurant. Or how strange it is to listen
to a baseball game on the radio that has
crowd noise piped in the public address
because no one is there in the stadium
because there are no tickets being sold.
I worry that my friends think of me like
a dog with a bad case of fear aggression.
But of course I won't bring it up to them.
I think I might feel better if I got some
work done—some writing, some music.
Or maybe it would just make things worse.
There are fleeting moments when I forget.
And I'm alive with my realms of being.
Before reality returns. This new living.
Is something burning? Is something here
on fire? It smells like something here is
burning or on fire. It might be in my head.

Archaeological Bells

They've buried the dreams underground, I think.
We don't seem to have them anymore, the dreams.
So I think it must be that someone disposed of them,
did away with them—maybe put them underground.

When we dig for the world that others left behind,
we find jewelry or tools—we sometimes find bells.
The bells no longer ring or make any kind of noise.
Perhaps they've been buried underground too long.
Like our dreams or visions. The other lives we live.

Sunset in the Rearview

Driving east away
from what my life was—
the sun hitting my mirror,
hurting my eyes.

Meet Me Where We Survive

It's only getting warmer. Even those who
don't want to admit it know that it's true.
I walked up the steps to use the restroom
and I was met with a pair of polar bears.
It was alarming to me, but they seemed
undisturbed—they didn't budge an inch.

I Wish I Hadn't

I hear it in the quieter moments of the night.
When all of the sirens have been put to bed
and there aren't any smoke detectors chirping
out my window and the world's still in its quiet
self-isolation. I hear it when the silent faces in
the darkness approach or else stare at me from
a distance, though even in the dark and without
my glasses on, I can still tell they are staring.
I can still tell that they are out there. Though
maybe they're not there. Maybe I'm hearing
things again. But I believe that it's something.
Something I can't ignore. A noise. A voice.
And I think that it's telling me to move on.

Ode to a Guy in a Guided by Voices T-Shirt Listening to Guided by Voices

When you love something
that isn't yourself or
something you created,
there are times when
you have to give in
utterly and completely
to that love, embrace
the magnitude of it,
sit right down and
drink a whole keg of it,
no regard for tomorrow.

A Voicemail from Jimmy

I know it will go away one of these days.
But for now, I still have it stashed away.
a voice message from two years ago.
It starts "Scott, this is Jimmy Cvetic."
Jimmy calling my phone while I was
likely still in bed. Leaving this voicemail
for me, saying, "I wanted to tell you that
I liked your book." Jimmy saying I have
nice style and saying that word "style"
like Bukowski, his hero. Jimmy says
it's a good book—"And I'm not saying
this to blow sunshine up your ass, ok?"
he says. Then the message winds down.
I know this old cell phone will one day
delete the voicemail or else not turn on
one morning, but for now I still have this
little bit of sound saved there, this moment
before he was gone. We've got his poems
and I have this voicemail. I have it saved.
For now. So that if I want to, I can hear
his voice again—maybe just once more.

Confessionalism II

for Bart

I stayed up late last night getting drunk by myself.
I put records on & filled a pipe as much as I liked.
I didn't feel bad about it. In fact, I felt pretty great.

What It Sounds Like in There

The other day, my friend Della asked me
what my brain is like. What it sounds like
in there. I described it as a geared engine—
park, neutral, drive, overdrive. My brain
being lodged in neutral most of the time.
But rolling down a hill. Or down a river,
maybe. I wasn't sure if it was working.

Phantosmia

Maybe it's just a trick
of my mind or something
but I swear sometimes
I can still smell
that scent of her
as if she were here,
right here next to me,
like that taste I get
of some strong bourbon
that I can still sense
in my system after
a night of a lot of it,
still lingering in me,
still intoxicating my brain.

Everybody's Got a Little Light Under the Sun

When I close my eyes, I can tell that there is light beyond them. "Who taught those fish to swim?" Who taught those birds how to warble?" My grandfather says these things to me as I wheel him to his room. And I don't know if he wants me to answer.

Blue Feeling

It's starting to come back again—that deep feeling.
I had it the other night, watching the documentary
about Larry that Phil lent me. I don't know how to
describe it exactly. If you have had it, you know it.

It burns deep inside of the body and it is similar to
feeling pain, though it is also different. It's a sort
of compulsion, maybe. Or else, a drive. To create,
to make something out of nothing. But I think it is
also the want to be a part of what it is that inspires.
The desire to share in the strange and beautiful of
that world of creation. The feeling of belonging it
can bring. The unexplainable relief of recognition
as something valuable or something understood.

That's what I felt when I watched all these people,
all these total strangers, talking on my TV screen,
talking about Larry, a man I never met but know.

Walt Whitman in a Little Pink Car

My friend Bart is letting his hair and beard grow out.
He tells me that it's his Transcendental Poet phase.
When he drives around town in his little pink car,
some people mistake him for Great Uncle Walt.
And they tell others that they saw Walt Whitman
driving a little pink car. Up there on Perry Highway.

Welcome Home and Don't Come Back

after Jason Irwin

There's a pine in a forest in a forest in a forest.
There's a fly in the house in the house in the house.
This is a nightmare inside a nightmare inside a nightmare.
But it's only a dream inside a dream inside a dream.

A Note from Kristin Naca Tucked in an Old Copy of *The Branch Will Not Break*

I know right where it is—in which room, on which bookcase and on which shelf of that bookcase. And that isn't always how it goes. Sometimes I'll scramble for hours in my place looking for a book, a record, or some small scrap of paper.

It's a first edition, ex-library, no dust jacket. And I believe my mother got it for me at John King in Downtown Detroit.

The bookplate on the front pastedown indicates that it was withdrawn from Marygrove College. The "Due Date" label on the rear flyleaf shows that the last checkout was in 1988.

I wonder now, in 2020, who decided to withdraw this book from the library back in the late 80s or early 90s, decided it to be a volume the library did not need on hand any longer.

Tucked in at "Lying in a Hammock…"—and of course at that poem—is Naca's short, handwritten note, scrawled in her neat cursive on the back of a scrapped photocopy from a book entitled *Transcendental Wordplay*. Her note reads,

"S.S.—The one day you're not around! ⊠ KNaca"

The note now must be over 15 years old—closing in on 20. It's just a little thing. A scrap of paper. A bookmark now.

But I love how it can remind me of those days years ago. The days and nights. Those memories. Of times far gone and away. Not to say that they were the best times ever. Just different. Just not now. Vivid images I can conjure— riding on the back of Naca's motorcycle on Fifth Avenue, or at a small party in some apartment dancing with Emily. Or maybe at Brandon's place with Bruce Lee looking on as Brandon did his impression of all four guys from U2.

Time, time. Always time. The world spins its ugly spins until it finds something beautiful again. And it carries on.

It carries on.

Everything's Unstable

Monday, early afternoon. Music playing in the other room.
I'm in the kitchen. On the table—a cup of coffee, folders,
some notebooks and some pens. The window is open.
September. Almost fall. And I'm feeling alright today.

That Dummy Has Nice Shoes

My buddy Irwin has an idea he tells me.
We are driving back from Kris's place,
where we were drinking Old Bushmills,
which Irwin calls "The Old Protestant,"
and Irwin spies a port-a-potty. "Do you
happen to know anyone who might own
a ventriloquist's dummy?" Irwin asks.
I tell him I would have to ask around.
"D'you see that Johnny-on-the-spot?"
he says, referring to the port-a-potty.
I tell him I do. So he tells me his idea,
which involves secretly stashing some
ventriloquist's dummy on the seat of
port-a-potty and watching the reaction
of the next person to use it. Naturally,
I look up ventriloquist dummies for sale.
I send a picture of a possible candidate
to Irwin and he replies, "That dummy
has nice shoes!" A promising candidate.

For Stefanie

Two big thunderstorms
in as many days—
sometimes you just get lucky.

5:45 in the Morning, Sudden Presence

for CA

I can't sleep. Woke up a little bit ago
from a dream of the dangers of driving,
a dash of work anxiety thrown in for fun.
The dream a sudden presence in the room,
something too large to put my arms around.

Then I start thinking. Never a good idea
at such a time. But I hit on some goodness.
You in my bed next to me in the sunlight
of early morning—the window behind us
open, with the screen in. You saying that
you heard birdsong you never heard before.
The birds and the rain. Train whistle far off.

And I starting mulling over all of the things
you said and did that I could thank you for.
Hoping that I have been grateful enough—
that I have shown my gratitude enough.

For dancing with me. For cooking for me.
For watching old movies with me. Driving
around town with the windows down and
Bud Powell playing through the car stereo.
Shopping for groceries together—finding
radishes and cucumbers, parsley, peppers,
fresh shrimp, half and half, good cheddar.

It's almost 6 a.m. now. And maybe you are
awake where you are too. I wanted you to
know that I bookmarked my favorite poems
by Frank O'Hara in the book I have for you.
I'll put it on the piano bench next to my bed.

Lime Life

I'm drinking Miller High Life cans with a very small wedge of lime stuck to them at the mouth. Sometimes the little hunk of lime falls in. I don't know why exactly I'm putting the little piece of fruit on my beer like that—I was never a "fruity beer" kinda guy. I guess because it's gotten hot, it feels like summer. The High Life cans are cheap down at the Wilkinsburg BevCo and I usually only like High Life ice-cold—as in, in a bucket or cooler of ice for hours. But I found a half-dead lime in the fridge and I decided that if I chopped off the bad part that I could save the rest and put little slices of it in my cheap High Life cans and pretend I was maybe drinking a Modelo or Tecate or Dos Equis, something imported, therefore fancy. I think it's working for me.

It's Over

Nobody to talk to, but that's ok. I've got these walls.
And this watered-down glass of something. I'm good
at this, I think. As long as I don't get thinking about this,
that, & the other. And if I do—well, my policy is to have
the thought, acknowledge it, & move on. Whether or not
that's a healthy way to deal with it, I can't say for certain.
But it's just how I am. I'm just trying to live—to survive.

I Dream a Highway, a Short Film

Early morning. The roar of big trucks
off in the distance out on the highway.

Interior—a bedroom awash in blue light.
A man and a woman on blue sheets.

The man is asleep—the woman awake.
On an electric piano, a small fan blows.

Where Do You Live Again?

I met Patty at the cemetery at 8 o'clock in the evening.
I didn't know exactly where I was going. But I found
Patty at the gates on Dallas, I parked, and we set out
for a walk. Patty told me that the fireflies should be
putting on a good show but that it wouldn't start for
an hour or two yet, so we'd have time to catch up.

We were in the city, but near the big park, so nature
was on display for us there in the cemetery—we saw
deer and turkey and even a fox, who crossed our path
in a loping fashion. We found a mausoleum tucked
back in a corner of the cemetery and set up shop on
the steps, breaking out beers and a little chocolate bar
Patty brought to share. There was some news to discuss,
but we started talking about our old friend, Tony, and
the stories about him started taking over. I told some
funny old stories about Tony and I was laughing and
before I knew it, I was crying and I didn't know if they
were tears of joy or grief but I guess it didn't matter.

The fireflies started up, just as Patty had promised
and so did the mosquitoes—I could feel them sucking
my blood out of me. Because it was June in Pittsburgh,
you could hear fireworks being shot off all around us.

And we talked about photographers for a while and I
told Patty about how my dad, a man of many hobbies,

had said that if he had pursued an artistic calling, it
would have been portrait photography. And we talked
about Teenie Harris and Patty said she once had a series
of Teenie Harris dreams and I thought about how once
I had a series of Richard Brautigan dreams for a while.

And I told Patty about my road trip to see the path of
The Johnstown Flood, from the manmade lake down
to the city of Johnstown and then up to the cemetery
high on the hillside with its massive monument
to the unknown dead. And then we talked about
David McCullough and about his great books.

And Patty asked me, "Where do you live again?"
and I laughed. It shouldn't have been a difficult
question to answer, but it was at that moment.

And when we left the cemetery, I got in my van
and rolled the window down so Patty could hear
the Ellington song on my stereo and I turned it up
and Patty started dancing there on Aylesboro Street,
dancing in the moonlight across from the cemetery.

Scott Silsbe was born in Detroit. He now lives in Wilkinsburg, Pennsylvania. His poems and prose have appeared in numerous periodicals and have been collected in the three books: *Unattended Fire, The River Underneath the City,* and *Muskrat Friday Dinner.* He is also an assistant editor at Low Ghost Press.